Flame Tree

Judith Kazantzis has had three earlier collections of poetry published: *Minefield* (Sidgwick & Jackson, 1977); *The Wicked Queen* (Sidgwick & Jackson, 1980); and *Let's Pretend* (Virago, 1984); and she shared *Touch Papers* (Allison & Busby, 1982) with Michèle Roberts and Michelene Wandor. In 1986 Bedlam Press published her political poem cycle *A Poem for Guatemala*.

She reads her poetry regularly at festivals, poetry societies, to students and other audiences, including in the USA. She is also a reviewer, short story writer, teacher and illustrator; an exhibition of her pictures (scraperboard, watercolour, and mixed media) was held in 1987 at the National Poetry Society Gallery.

Judith Kazantzis was born in 1940. She has lived in London and southern England and recently in Key West, USA, during the winter. She lives with the American writer Irving Weinman. Her daughter and son are in their twenties.

Judith Kazantzis
Flame Tree

Methuen

A Methuen Paperback

FLAME TREE
British Library Cataloguing in Publication Data

Kazantzis, Judith
   Flame tree.
   I. Title
   821'.914   PR6061.A98

   ISBN 0-413-17880-3

First published in Great Britain 1988
by Methuen London Ltd
11 New Fetter Lane, London EC4P 4EE
Copyright © Judith Kazantzis 1988

Photoset by Rowland Phototypesetting Ltd,
Bury St Edmunds, Suffolk
Printed and bound in Great Britain
by Cox and Wyman Ltd, Reading, Berks.

Some of these poems have appeared in *Ambit,
Angels of Fire Anthology, City Limits,
The Green Book Anthology, The Honest Ulsterman,
Literary Review, Ninth Decade, Other Poetry,
The Pen* (Eng. Centre, Intnl., PEN), *Purple and
Green Anthology, The Rialto, Solares Hill* (USA),
*Stand, Stride, Verse, With a Poet's Eye
Anthology, Writing Women.*

For my mother and my father,
for the pleasure of their loving company

Contents

The best world is the body's world
filled with creatures   filled with dread
misshapen   yet the best we have
our raft among the abstract worlds
and how I longed to live on this earth
walking her boundaries   never counting the cost

from 'Contradictions: tracking poems',
Your native land, your life, Adrienne Rich
(WW Norton 1986; British edition 1986)

A little medley for Civil Defence

The withering geraniums,
under one red clothes peg
on the line,
stiffen and snake up to the lightning.

One clothes peg and nothing
on it, sharp scarlet; we
brought in the clothes and the –
olios, olios, shouted the stormwarner.

I walk to the harbour
under sentence of lightning.
Ships, boats tremble there,
water pinned flat

by dot on dot of rain,
by its blue grey surges
pulsing across – catching
me – I run back in the gusts.

Over our aged olive tree,
our cobbled roof,
sort of ours for four weeks . . .
the sky booms, overhead

and far off softly:
in a cyclone's ring, round
the silver ravines around Lakka.
Then, finally, this

crustacean, thickened grey sky,
opens its wings.
The sun is bare, before dusk,
sharp gold, you'd think motionless.

olios *means 'all'.*

My mother's house

Doves, crying to each other
raucous and moody —
doves flash past the
windows, yearning —

circle the topmost pines.
One, trapped in the
green fir tunnel by
the tennis court

pants and crashes on
the netting, its fan
tail quilled a stiff oyster
shell rosy grey

till it ricochets
out, and flees on through
a sunbeam I saw
in a child's book

of the Holy Land.
A German Christ child
bouncing with gold hair
across a field of roses

daisies and cornflowers
to the Garden of Evening:
black shadows and doves
white on a crude cypress.

Clinging is fire, the sun, the middle daughter.
It means coats of mail and helmets.
It means lances and weapons.
What does the armourer say? The riddling
of the lance, bending, crushing,
smoothing out to gleaming. A ring of hammers
their drip and spark out and down.
Among men it means the big bellied.

It is the sign of dryness. They say it is
the tortoise, the crab, the mussel, the hawkbill tortoise.
Belly slow, beak moving prudently among dry
grasses, this way and that.
Imagine the snail and its sister the crab from
the thin ebb, wandering on the floor by
the armourer's dirty foot. How would
they find their way out? How to avoid
the dark fire? the hammer blow? They crawl
into a belly of ashes. Meanwhile the maker
of helmets clings to the dead article he knows
because of its beauty.
The black blue case of a mussel is
trivial, the wrapping box of a delicacy. But I worship
its motionless changing colours.
They say among trees
it means those which dry out in the upper
part of the trunk.
Thick headed. Small brains. Hair pulled round nothing.
Dry, the middle daughter knows the
sputter of the unmaking fire: its grunting timber yard
its beach of calcined shells and houses of lower forms.
She knows the rocketeer's ambition
he concentrates in a lance momentarily
incandescent.

Pandora, maker of boxes
made of bamboo, made of woven palm fronds
made of brass and sheets of dimpled copper
tinged green, rollicking with elephants and
                              a tasselled script

Made of thistledown and dandelion, clock weights
balanced by wind   Made of spray, catspittle and
                              seed dust
                    her boxes of seeds
rattling, flattened, hollow-tubed, pointed, dark red

Of pebbles the dark blue of the white cat's-eyes
lacquered up and glued to boards of cheap ply
                              held feebly by tin-handed clasps
Adorned with the nautilus: in the sailboat of the nautilus
the child goes splashing, dipping her hands
into the dawn and the sea channel
              one radiance sliding over another

Made of alphabets, scallops, clams, turkeywings,
    sundials
the ocean structure, the thinnest bones and the coarsest

Pandora alabaster of whatever is inside
throws open to your invitation, sits back and watches
                              while you throw

the gouged void of six walls to the ground

What should she say? Box always within a box
always inside a box, solid or salt sea, made of your
painful rage, whatever there is to hand It holds
                              whatever is inside
that shines or lies low or sings softly

Lifting a thousand lids, how will you
open the six walls of void? How will you know
                    what it is inside
that suns the quartz at dawn or lies low
or shouts a pitch
                    like a robin in the naked garden.

Mother

'. . . all men are Noah's sons.'
Richard Wilbur — from *Still Citizen Sparrow*

Mrs Noah was a little dimmer.
Not Bible fact but a mediaeval
scold who'd have got ducked
if she'd raised her village tongue
the way she did on board the ark.

Not my mother, this pauper myth
of husbands. Can't see her my mentor.
Can't think any woman I know
would like this scratcher either
cut off from powerful speech with God.

Pedant angel pinhead me!
Richard Wilbur means, we women
are included among Noah's sons.
Sons include daughters, and men naturally
include women, so we are also Noah's sons.

And this means, hanging loose, that
Mrs Noah was really Mr Noah himself,
very noble and worth copying of course
so anywhichway you and I are born of Noah
and we all had penises before the Flood.

'The Saltonstall Family' by David Des Granges

c. 1636–37* – the Tate Gallery, London

The strangest family portrait I ever saw.
Six members: two children, a baby
a man and two women compose it.
Two children on the left
link hands to a troubled father
whose free hand, in a white glove
hooks back a rich chrysanthemum red
stage curtain; in fact a bed curtain.

Behind these folds and his golden
doublet and their red brocaded
dresses lies the mother, slack mouthed
and shroud faced as the ghost
she was by the year the artist came.
And to the right hand front –
decorously she holds her own infant,
the stepmother, the second wife.

The stepmother of the children
sits in a castle of satin, fold
building on fold. Her young
ringletted face guards sincere
duty done, pride and unease.
Her boy is bound like a dahlia
bud in red and gold. She's
model for a stepdaughter, bride white.

The mother dying looks with eyes
dark, bright, detached – delirious?
back at her little pair. She stares
round her husband, too far gone
to be sincere; just stares. Out of
her time, dazed. Once more
she empties her cumbrous fingers
to bless, to give him those lives.

So I'm circled back to see how
his own linked hand ushers these
children across to the second wife.
He looks at her across the inset
phantom – How to interpret this
look? Sensual, or proud or grateful?
Or, his eyebrows delicate under
the crowned hat and the massed hair,

a withdrawn relief at sincere duty
done? In any event his gaze
travels out past the woman,
I see now. And I am angry at how
this man, in his domestic love,
grew master of sad histories
manager of life, and death and births
his players growing devout or dead.

And also happy. See the child
the older one. Leaning, swaying
she gazes straight (the only one)
at our naive and honest painter
Master Des Granges, who's weaving a
pretty idyll to keep her still.
She's bursting with giggles and 'Sir
I shan't believe you!' There, dancing
she stands, pursemouthed and brilliant-
eyed, holding her father's hand.

                *   *   *

Except, I've made a mistake.
This vivid 'girl' is a boy really
in petticoats still but, look,
no apron. Unlike the small sister
stout, stoic and white bibbed,
held quiet at this brother's hand.

So now this boy, swaying
and brilliant-eyed: he requires
another story altogether.
Des Granges leaves the dance of Flora
to thunder of bat-eyed monsters
and wars. 'I'll slay you dragons!'
the boy calls out his shining
promise, holding his father's hand.

As for the girl with no apron,
who was my own ghost in a family
portrait spooky with right habit,
she tries to exist after all.
Her form shining under the boy's.
A possibility interred.
And she is the saddest ghost truth of
her mother, unpainted, unheard of.

* _Originally known as 'The Bedside Farewell', the Saltonstall family portrait turns out to be more unusual than the death in childbed of one seventeenth-century wife. Expert dating now suggests two wives present, not one . . . the first Mrs Saltonstall died in 1630 shortly after and quite likely as a result of her third childbirth. (Her two elder and surviving children are pictured as they were at that date.)_

'Madame Boucher' by Boucher
– the Frick collection, New York

Madame Boucher has
black eyebrows, a tight waist,
pink satin slippers. Silks,
ribbons, bags all over the floor.

Monsieur Boucher set up
this *déshabillé* with hand
akimbo satisfaction. The mending
on the stool, the tassels
twining from the drawer.
A la mode a little robed
ample stomached Chinaman
squats on the wall cabinet
over the pink chaise-longue.
His rose and white skinned
apple of a household slut.
She compresses her mouth shut.
And half smiles when Boucher
looks up; her brows are black,
her large hand rests her head.
She is thinking of noons,
of rides in the Tuileries and of
less careful eyes; also
of her subtle soup the maid
is simmering dry while
she's set simpering
on the chaise-longue; or simply
of lobbing the affable Buddha
through the long tulle robed
windows that look on the Tuileries.
Tu es dans la lune, he smiles.
Her great jet eyes slide
away and she half smiles.

She'll make his soup –
her lovers, maybe. Their bliss,
her beauty and his genius,
chez Boucher that's the picture.

There were then three Victorian men
                    and a nanny
And the Lord said to the nanny
Arise and take these Victorian men

One by one and from behind
and seated on top and unto the third hour
When I shall come again
And you shall hear the cock crow three times.

And the nanny arose
and went down into the men
and the men arose
and went down into the nanny

And the Lord said
Now am I satisfied with my nanny
            and my Victorian men.

                    (Cor !!)

His little girl feeds Daddy
TV preview of Budget Day in the eighties

Here's
a sight of the boar
head in closeup, mounted
stuffed on a wall, relaxed
before his tusking of
widows, disabled, geriatrics . . .
        Freckledy
not Heath pink but teacup
rose and cream, rolly fleshed,
prince never more, the
broad muzzle juts out:
today he's just Daddy Bearkins.
On the great knee sits
Goldilocks, plaited, clean-
eared, muslinned, she's
in no danger, she's no orphan.
        The face
above works pink
lips to stretch sleepily
wide and to smile on his little
love.   She turns her slender
shoulder, twists up and . . .
into her Daddy Bear's
maw, over short teeth,
across a lower lip
maintained replete on chins,
she passes a sugary bik;
            the face
is almost too stuffed
to chew. Is thus
kept going, on extract of
millions of such small fry
— a consumer of such
prodigious hypnotic suction,
it could claim the victims
place themselves in
                the gullet

of the face and close
the jaws behind them.

This lumbering face
    can charge

Sciatica in Esher in 1984

Even the Scargill foamers
    are speechless suddenly
over their potty azaleas – flower
    of the luxurious South East
or of acid Scottish hotels.

They are carried screaming
    like wets or wimps on
boards to bed for six weeks.

They look pale and stern as
    the Great War, as they go in
to be skewered and fused.

They can't blame the miners
    for slipped discs and stuffed
bellies over the azaleas, though
    they would like to.

For example Owen

A question to four deaths:
Wilfred Owen, France 1918;
Ernst Tauber, France 1918;
David Tinker, off the Falklands 1982;
Armando Souda, off the Falklands 1982

An officer, a good shepherd
who thought he should go
with his doomed flock, with love.
He asked, how could he sit in comfort
even in conscience and inside prison
while his men passed in their thousands
under the hand of the giant into the cave.
So he went back in there. He 'went west'.
A bullet smashed him on a canal bank
a week before Armistice.
The very bridge (over the Sambre)
was never built that his men
tried to build. Almost all of them
were 'casualties'. He was 'struck'
while 'calmly' helping to fix the
duckboards into place. There,
Owen handed himself into the war.
He 'fell' among planks awash,
hit and hit, smashed, gouged into
springing arrowhead shards under
the fire; by virtue of a crafty
self-deceit, by reason of a huge desire
for a virtuous reason to live, out of purest
nobility; among debris slithering
across Lethe, planks drifting waterlogged
and sideways, batted by each other,
nudged by shapes hunched underwater
like giants; he fell down among
matchsticks carrying the random and
slumped dead making a crossing.

Planks for white crosses
like plague signs stuck up forever
and tended, as if the crushing plague

might lift, one day, from our houses
if the signs are kept fresh
and we remember.

We don't forget.
The lethal courage of the lamb.
Our bloodgeld two wars long.

From old colonial days
a malaria flickers underskin
a muttering sootfall
of sorrow and love, hate and revenge
upworded to the old noble
pro patria decorum est . . . Gasbag
speeches unworded to the pure brass blare
of Downing Street. Upcoding into
computers, signals, radar, rockets, missiles
and three torpedoes
to hit, hit, hit
'a likely violation of the exclusion zone'.

By Sambre
they hadn't invented bodybags
with plastic zips. Stretchers they had.

'"All a poet can do today is warn."'
With what caught pride does the young
officer draw up to his peaked cap.
In the photograph
Owen smiles with his expressive
eyes and his plump cheeks. In the next,
a glad, rangy face, fair hair,
David Tinker, Lieut. RN, on board, ploughing
the South Atlantic, at first ardent,
then writing home, '"the professional forces
of both sides"' — he was one —

'"do what they are told. If two
megalomaniac idiots tell them
to beat each other's brains out they do."'
A week later an Exocet
'beat its way' to his cruiser.
Among those burned to death was Tinker.
'To the end he was calm and brave.'
Tinker, David . . . soldier, sailor. Souda, Armando.
Tauber, Ernst. Owen, Wilfred. Smiles. Rictus.
Caught in smiles, some. Zipped up.
Flown home to a salute. Interred. Crossed white.
With what ritual pride does the young
officer draw up to his peaked cap.

'"My subject is War and the pity
of war"' . . . Owen
Tinker . . . Tauber . . . Souda
O passionate lovers of the public virtue
O young wisemen of pity,
how is it, deftly, deftly, you kill
but yourselves only? The flatterers
salute you out.

You golden fleecy flock, why run
before the brokers and the farmers of blood?
They buy and sell in tender carcases
on war's slab, and in between
in peace – they speculate in futures.
While the young rams breed up
glittering with a hard urge to wrestle death.

The flatterers have released you
among the stumps of French woods or on
sheep islands among cavelike seas –
Here are the high-powered assault rifles
the heat-sensing missiles entirely

under your hands —
Turn round, look round behind you.
See them sitting comfortably behind you
in their bunkers, on silk chairs.
There they work.
They sail corpses like paper boats.
Make another formation, brothers —
Lock your sights — Advance
on these rears — satiny rear ends.
Your words become your weapons, your weapons
are your words; roaring across the ceremonial grounds;
saying this to them: Halt!
                    No more your burden beasts!
                    Our missiles lick your arses!
                    No more death trumpeting and
                        trumpeting.
                    No more.

You must say it to your flatterers.

Turn, soldiers of unfreedom, look round.
We who love you, who are your own people
we offer a docile back-up
to those who farm your deaths —
Turn and curse us
out of our timidly ranked houses
from which we offer you up.

But you say: Orders are orders.
But you say: I cannot leave my men, my brothers.
But you say: Now this is my only life
                so has to be my death.
                No one at home can know our deep bonds.

I shout back through the dumb wood
across the bloody channels:

You are the soldiers, not them.
Envisage a life, not a death
in brotherhood – is that impossible to men?
This question is for you.
You are tied to a killing post by garlands
marvellous and phantom as poems.
Whip vines or gossamer, what garland ties
you to your killing post?
Which one, steel or breakable?
This question is for you.

Owen . . . Tauber . . . Tinker . . . Souda
it was the question I burned to ask
of the brave shepherds, the brave sheep, dead mutton.

It is not we

            Bam!
        And that felt good.
And I wanted more
        I wanted more
                y'know

I wanted to go
        out and kill some
            Gooks
        I wanted to go out
            and kill some
                    Gooks
                        y'know

no more than a fly

Hey jet, get 'em and
        that felt good and
            hey jet, get 'em
        and that felt good
and the napalm just dripping off 'em

You take them

My heart just soared
I turned round and looked
                    at them
My heart just soared
a bloody good bunch of killers

May you be winners, more
Importantly
in the Biggest Game of All/Life/
Which we All Play

The daily grind   ★   I enjoy it

It was a pretty country
except for the people

     This shitty piece of ground
         I'm dying
              and I can't fucking believe it.

. . . not we
              who are the savages
the lives of my countrymen
              are worth no more than a fly
it is not we
You take them
              and swat them
                    dead
and that's that   *who are the savages*
     that's that

     I'm dying
and I can't fucking believe it.

A little medley for Civil Defence
Duck and Cover – United States CD slogan
Protect and Survive – British CD slogan

Ducks and survive
waddle to the gangplank
looking for grub in the bank.
Underground the steak smoulders,
the wine grows body, the Cadillac steams.
On top of living we survive
or subvive, or not we
but a few – d'you know them?

A harmless day at Greenham

A harmless day at Greenham.
One soldier behind the Orange gate
eyeing his toe, looking
as gloomy as a black pudding.

A cloud bank of that sagging grey
peculiar to English Novembers.
A barrelled fence of snarled erections
containing not much, a couple

of logo towers, a mound or two
of burial chambers. I've read
they call them silos, as if
they held wheat. Outside

the colour of a woman's long scarf —
a woollen rainbow. Mud. Cold.
A fire, with chipped planks and
furze. A kettle we must hide

from the Government. Twice
a day it steals pots and pans.

**Flame tree   the Amazon expedition of
the famous naturalist Louis Agassiz, 1862—63**

1

Madame Agassiz
in her own right is an angel,
so says William James, expedition member.
She stands vivid but sweaty
propped and *soigné* in skirt upon skirt
— for Alexandrina is her speed.
She peels her blue eyes for some aerial petal
on which to float the senses
under the net these long river nights
noisy with whoops and whistles.
Natural hope, but there he is flat out
what with all day the natural world.

Her name has not much to do with tropic forests
or the leap of monkeys up tree trunks
beasts to which her mistress compares her:
Look, Alexandrina! Up. Up. There! Go fetch
the flowering branch.

          . . . The servant's hair
is a great coiffeured Afro, a stately frame
to her rococo mouth and lucent barricaded gaze.
'. . . having,' writes Madame facing,
'in her extraordinary hair standing out
all round her head the mixture
of the two races, the Indian length
combined with the Negro crispness.'
Her use, apart from blossom brought down
to blotter, is to prepare skeletons
of fish caught in the Amazon
for Monsieur to christen, stick and stuff.
The account says nothing else.

Named for a library ticket out of old Egypt.
What was her family?
Name of a white conqueror of speed.
Dwindled to 'drina', to suit the 'monkey-like' girl
who 'intelligently' typed the bones.
The woman, her hardy skeleton
long gone through earth to transmutation
into the auras that rock by day
over the forests of Brazil –
she has rendered the passion flower and the trumpet
    vine,
the wood of life, flame of the wood, flame tree,
shower of orchids; she has named the river's force
into which under leaves: a tributary: one of millions:
her supplanted name has poured.

2

The hardwood tree grows tall
by grace of the clouds.
The vapour floats above the fountain trees,
result, cause, ascending, falling.
How the mists feint and fold away
secretly the moth, the toucan, the spider, the jaguar.
'I shall never cease,' wrote the young Agassiz
'to consecrate my whole energy
to the study of nature; its powerful
charms have taken . . . such possession
of me . . . I shall always sacrifice
everything to it.'

3

Monsieur Agassiz
has gone home to applause;
the decks of his steamers are waist high in flesh;
120 species, of which ⅔ are 'unknown'.
Who follows the sage of fish?
The naturalists of São Paulo, Rio, Miami and Houston
are out collecting. This will take time.
It is projected, with luck and capital
and labour and demand, in 35 years
Amazonia will be collected. In short
a crisp sacrifice in the making
for the great great grandchildren
of the woman of extraordinary hair.
They are as thin as gar and do not now
shin up trees in the country of monkeys.

The botanist sees the 100 foot tree.
The botanist saws the 100 foot tree.
Here is a new
              playground.
                          Here are
                              the playboys.
        The tree becomes a
                      two by four.
                              See.
                                Saw.

Bauxite, manganese, petroleum, gold.
Come, disperse these mists!
Till nothing's there to support their witness.
Let the valuable geologist dig his garden.

Ash and Senhor Ass the consecrator
(Come, disperse these mists!)
prepare a skeleton.
Let the valuable geologist dig his garden.

Till nothing is there to support their witness.
Come, disperse these mists.

Finally: Ethiopia

people arriving in their thousands
many of them on the verge of death.

Heavy rain throughout today
but with bright intervals.

That's the news and weather
at ten past nine.

This week's composer Dvořák
took much of his inspiration

from Slavic folk melodies

plaintive rhythms, evoking
the sufferings of generations

yet also acceptance, with its
wistful, ultimately consoling resolution.

Key West

Sonny Rollins
stood on Brooklyn Bridge
for four years
and blew and blew   figuring
this and that
after Bird died   and
                                until
he was clear to walk forward again.

They say you could hear the sax
groaning and crying
above the percussions of the cars
and the barely pounding bass
        wind over the East River
            all day fisting
        across one thousand cables

Like a feather
        brushing sunlight
            On its own   until

it came for earth again

flew   like silver in a cool fever
                into Manhattan.

                        New York

All night long in Brooklyn

Cop cars squeal, howl and gasp
across the grid pattern. In my sleep
huge worms fight at intersections,
clapping and batting their brazen wings:
a Clang . . . Clang, sprouting inside
the two beat squeal. These
are the fire-engines come
swinging. Around this neck of
the brownstones and the big Navy
blocks we're a tiltyard all night
for dragons and marshals. They use
the breezy hours to boom and
yowl, yah! yah! over each crossing.
The sleepers, packed upstairs and stairs,
like steers, or peasants
are to be kept a shade edgy:
on their feet, shadow danced;
malleable, or anyway a shade
deferential, on sidewalks
glass crazed: wing
upon wing of dreamers.

Which goddesses are YOU?
— book advertisement in
Women's Review of Books, New York

Not so damn easy to find
the strange one, that one
without gender or tissue
who must clench fists

Easier to have fun with
Athena, Aphrodite
Hera; be wise Thursdays,
my thighs sticky wide

all weekend, and
on Mondays hang out
the washing, and the
straightforward Joves down

side up to cool off.
But for iron days and water days
like Wednesdays or the
unsexed passage of

time, where are the fists
of the strange one?
Curled like runts so
tight inside; not godlikely

to sculpt a drip drip
or smash these iron gutters of days.

In the middle of Fort Lauderdale

In the middle of Fort Lauderdale
where retired skippers
sit, thighs wide, on flowered settees
growing plumper
flicking over the channels
in the hurricane season
saying, did they mention a tropic high?
while the rain pours straight down
through the two palms, one
on each side of the pool in the yard.

The manatees rise
mermaid and merman,
every five minutes they rise for air,
snorting through their moustaches,
easing their oil brown bellies
in the heat crashing
off the concrete walls of Port Everglades;
again ruddering into the
conduit and its warm and nutritious
sludge, on platypus tails, those
famous travellers' tails.

      The mermaid
does she hide her hairy mouth
and sing all moon long
upon a white oil drum among
hushed slicks.
The concrete's thick as the earth.
It surely goes down to China.

      As for the old seacows
gallantly they burbled inland,
their voyage of exploration
and discovery.
A company streamed after: cyan blue

and xanthic yellow angel-fish;
even a ray, a curling triangle
flaps off beneath the slick.
The parrot-fish bathe in oil.
A rat hunches across the bank
and a Great White Heron refrains
for hours on one leg.

The plump blue and yellow angels
flex flat, sideways
up the concrete, almost
in air, to get at the crumbs
the skipper has just thrown. He
snorts out of his Oldsmobile
for five minutes: let me say,
it's better than Oceanworld, you
don't pay and every show's different.

And let me tell you, for my
second career, I'm going up.
Up. Hot air balloon
chartering, probably
over Mexico. I know the
winds, after forty years
at sea; and I've had the sea.
Dotty will follow with
champagne and caviare packed on ice.
Etc. We think
the Cadillac will get up
most mountains.

       Stop, here!
– the liquor store. I have
a Marlene Dietrich video I taped and
we can get smashed after supper
over her legs, and her age.

Gulf shallows
— off Key West

I pulled taut an edgy sloe horizon
of rough cloud and full sea.
It banded like a runner's tape.
                    Today
the sun clarifies and clarifies, an agent;
brimful and deceitful in fact.
The sea flares from the speedboat
for marathons, where cormorants
with muscular wings graph
the fields moving, neck and
belly to wave, executors
of my eye. Runners who vanish.
Some place they leave, at or before the edge
where the jade and milky blue and
silvered and opal ranges wash through
the cordon and sky can't be sky,
where the edge had been, so I was clear.

My eyes idle. I can't impose or construct.
The blue fields I drafted have preceded
I blank out into the escaping, where
am I heading
                        species   orders
      kingdoms

                  sun deceiver   sea   lies

The hoop that barrelled the sun
is it intact, unburst
by the fermentations, is there the
sloe blue circle, like a quoit
around us, underneath or behind
the white games of the sun?

I catch the hot red of my eyelid.
The colourless wink of a butterfly
scrapes and flickers: eyelashes
pause, whatever I see, across
my retinas like the veins of wings,
the legs of a new insect
uncramping and disentangling before it
delivers itself from gauze and fluid
and prances out of eyesight
into a flimsy dabble
                              a black drop
            a nearly transparent stopper of air

Barracuda

Under a pall of crisp fruited
orange stemmed seaweed
hangs the sea tiger.
A white substantial flank.
My head's half turned in
its mask, scoping the green
halls of six foot water, nearly
empty halls stretching all ways
over dark rush beds,
odd convoys of pale snappers
in threes or fours, wandering
half visible. I was edging
to my right against the waves
to circle the weed mat
with its cloudy undershadow.
I was seawise in my simple
dislike. In and out of my eye's
jump I caught its long hull
striped, unstirring, silver, attentive.

It lies suspended on the shadowed
side of the pier, or by a rock
wasting time and my nerves
and doing nothing; like a
stuffed white and charcoal striped
pike someone caught and mounted
on the dark chimney breast high
over the mantel and under
the heavy vine of the moulding.
The mirror over the mantelpiece
runs without a word into a salt
hall of shifts and screens.
And out of the folds on to
a retina gawping and flickering
away as I curve for the light
clamps an eye, a lip, a jaw.

The obsession
slides under the sea clusters.

But the barracuda lying in
half dark under the shadow of
the weed is no one's mania:
a spurious mirror image
for our shifts and screens.
It rocks back and forth, idling,
smiling the bad conscience smile
which is a phoney . . .   Except
for sure it scares what's larger,
white tentacled: me.
Smart that first pike
who pulled its dirty meaningful grin
and knew it was meaningful.
The plainer truth is, that recessed lip
supports a raft of teeth.
Do something stupid such as
tease the fish, or such as spear
another fish with this one around
and the scent flowing will launch
it right in without respect of bodies.
Let be however —
(and wear no metal in the water
like a silver pass of fish scales
in case of error —) Let be:
it won't flee, but invisibly
back off and surrender path, then
watch and hang again.

I flap past with ray-like calm.
A slight eyewhite tremor inside
the mask — a quick confession of sins
autonomic in a minute swerve.
Girl, that's it, I do not wound

nor do I offer the shine of a wound.
Not a stomach knot more
now that I know this
barracuda like a blood relation.

Like a little nodding mandarin
Anna, sun faced, brown buttered
entices me to her cottage room
by a blue velvet pool.

She lies back, slender and floppy,
nothing to do all day
all summer in the ferocious heat;
her dark brown hair curls wet

against her boatwoman tan,
against her dark child's eyes.
She tells me of her 'tresora',
I dive, she says, and giggles.

An old Black woman

                              sits in a middling

                              blue print dress

            sits rocking

Crickets tap tin spoons.

Two powered male basses

                    New Age humdinging

                              the Sunday noon

            hereabouts not a soul

Lustral   air-stunners   party-givers.

Three Christmas palms

                    fronting her yard

                         are bound in blue

            and in silver

On her nape her grey hair inclines to a bun.

Psalm of tinsel

                    binding the trunks

                    spiralling into the trunks

                    of spiral streamers

Plumb   of tornado air.

Roof rats also nest in palms.
When the coconuts are ready,
to the annoyance of the owner
who has sat in his apartment below
with the TV and a crate of Milwaukee
all these months,
the rats drill into the shaggy heads
to suck the thin milk.   Over the husks
they twine, sucking.
They spreadeagle their pink hands.

For other food or for the moonlight
they cruise below.
They hare over the downlands
of silver gables tiled in aluminium.
They jump down by disordered hair,
the wiry plaits and hanks of ficus branches
bell pulls passing upper veranda
to lower veranda, home of a white turret
the boudoir of Mrs Carrasco;
or the crazy cottage next door,
its gate of hen wire,
its propped car – 'This car is not abandoned'
its plastic pelican, its Milwaukee man.

And so to the windy pavement
where the green coconuts blow down.

They bang, now and then, in the night.
They roll in among the seamed brown ones
piling the dry, blossom filled gutters.

Nature, at Fort Taylor Point

A dolphin leapt out before the sun.
Black and bent and plump. Away
in the channel beyond the stumps of rocks.
A plump bow, a fat forked tail, and in.

You teased me and vowed, 'you're back
with fucking Flipper again.' 'Idiot,'
I said, 'you curse at enthusiasms
you haven't the passionate love of natural

things, like fish, to share.' And the wild
dolphin, returning to the turquoise coloured
sea before the down-setting sun of
January, broke out ripples, on and on.

Till thirty minutes at least after the herd
had gone, you slid by whistling and grinning:
'Dolphins, my nature's love, aren't fish,'
and blocked off the sunset with a kiss.

And my son slept in the sitting-room
when he stayed with us

You lay under a creamy, baby soft blanket.
Your shoulders were, morning after morning,
cinnamon brown, loose, large and patched
red where the sun had broiled you out
cycling. Against our clinking and padding,
door latches, the toilet, coffee ticking, the
swish of the rowing machine on the deck
you dug into sleep. Your hair was salty
and wavy, punk cut, stiff with sea –
its glimmering coral and tangleweed long cut –

I cut across the other side to the bathroom
seriously quiet, a mother who tried
to leave your dreaming alone. But
this midnight I look back to the wall
where the sofa hogs its old place and the couch
is gone, like you only a few hours
of silence ago. I know I could never,
should never, have stroked your face
or stiff hair, or sat down to hold you –
Unthinkable, Phaedra or Jocasta woman!

Still, an aura of you, sulky, reserved
in thought, by now unbiddable adult being
might be said sleepily to linger around.
And it circles poor Phaedra on;
if only for a wish, the frown magicked;
if only for that tendril of the
old smile you snaked out shyly after
my shy last kisses: the scarce whisper:

'physically I am alone, touch me a little
though I'll back and hurl stones on you from
behind my rock, for I'm well aware of
Jocasta, of Phaedra and of course Medusa
O glint-haired mother – But touch me a
little, at the forking of the ways.'

There was a fierce earthquake under the island
of Ithaca once, like a couple of cats
or maybe big rats rummaging among the pilings
of the house here, thousands of miles away
in the isle of mopeds and palm trees. Ithaca
too has mopeds. Yesterday the bend among
small pines of a country road, unfenced
through low white rocks, pine needles and myrtle
cornering a bluff over turquoise water.
This flickered by in mind as soft as olives
run the sun through their discreet leaves;
as chancy, for I couldn't recall where or
how low were the pines, how soon the grove.
I was padding along in flip-flops, in summer.
Am I to smoothe such gentle disturbances over
and not be sad for silver-tongued leaves
and the coruscated body of the olive tree?
I sometimes have thought, I'll never see it again,
the elderly one, who can alter sunlight.

To go down Love Lane
you have to walk through the debris
first, which are rotting palm fronds, a pile,
and four lidless garbage cans, green and brown,
brimfull. The thin orange cat hangs
half in and the little black dog
drags a bag full of tins and Kentucky fries
sweet with ash and ants and the runny slide
of fast food out onto the parking lot
and goes to sleep and the sun gets stronger
and stronger.

            You and I walk down,
walk weightless or nearly so in the pool
underneath the small palms and the bougainvillea,
the nonstop red and purple and scarlet flowers.
My vagina is full of you and
you are laughing and so am I,
your hands pulling me back, your hands
your palms hold me by my breasts
gently easing me back onto you;
on the contrary your lips from above
the wide wet lips of a genial husky —
a merdog up from the beach . . .
over my cheekbones, over like a bunch of ripples,
over my plastered eyebrows, neat bones,
my hair rattails, mouth laughing, open wide
riding your human cock and your mouth
biting your swishing hands, under
the fronds, unable to stop laughing,
under the fence, under a tin lid of heat
vanished off me, drawn skyward
the constant pressure; that time no
coming down, no it was I going out
airily with you, in company with you, in
myself, I in water and freely within
and having scope, land and light strength
to move in all ways.

Preacher Egan's sermon
– an anecdote of old Key West

'Know ye not that they
which run a race run all
but one receiveth the prize?'
Thundering on this text
Preacher Egan, one Sunday
in the old Courthouse used
for church on Key West.
This piratical respectable kingdom
of a genteel tropic island
was, so he would groan
an Augean Stables to cleanse
(he had some Greek) . . . today
ramming it home, God's
was the prime and apex product
to be had by the free
competition which (when
fairly pursued by the free)
had made their isle
so golden and
lovely a home. His flock
nodded: a shoal
that grazed on the sea reefs
prosperously all week
for falling gold:
snappers in stiff gills, espoused
to angel-fish on the sidelines
floating in silken
                          hoops.
Back
from the law house
on its coral promontory
ranged the white verandas
of these wellmannered creatures,
fanned all hurricane and
heat through, by lustrous
silver thatch palms, also
                          by slaves.

Preacher
Egan, in the raising of
his hands for the last
cleaning up exhortation,
                              paused.
Beyond
          the white limewood door
hung the sea, like a peacock's
eye in a box.
There, in mid Word, he glimpsed
a black speck, with tangled
outriding arms
like an insect swimming in the eye.
He frowned and saw a schooner
with smashed masts
juddering on the eye's pupil,
a dark bar of mangrove swamp
they called Crawfish Key:
antennae of the long
reefs lying under
those hushed
God turned Key Westers that
                              Sunday of grace.

It was Sunday
                as said
yet humans cried in the fated
ship for salvage;
Preacher Egan paused, as said
— were they, drowning
body and soul, less to be saved
then the faces in ringlet and
whisker before him
who were merely drowning in soul?
He opened his mouth to
cry loudly 'shipwreck', for crimp
and sideburn, all were turned to

him; only the tall Preacher
could see the sea and the
mote in its eye – he shouted
to them eloquently
and at great length renewing
his text, that all
                      run for God –
They sat
up again, reticule and pocket watch
shut again, admiring
this fresh brilliance just when
his light had been fading . . . like
their own sun setting, the
ball of gold dripping and
then out of its pale afterglow
the wonderful, inflammatory corona.
So he expounded, moving
them, and moving down the aisle.
His large cheeks shone with
                              sweat:
like
a hermit crab seeking a new shell
(enthused eyeballs fixed
on the bench of town elders,
sharks in tall white cravats
and curly grandfatherly beards, all
wellknown to Preacher Egan . . . so
that they stared back, pinched
in his spell) he moved so
in a fervent sideways
sort of skip. Then reached, still
preaching, the wide open white door.
                      And paused.

They had
          twirled slowly
right round on their tails.

'Know ye not that they
which runneth a race run all –'
They saw their longlegged pastor
in black silhouette against
the peacock sea.   Beyond his ear
Crawfish Key crawled, a dark
blur, and entangled
in the faraway froth
around it a tiny waving
heap of
masts, sheets, shrouds
                              and spars.

'But one receiveth the prize!'
and Preacher Egan hollering
'shipwreck' turned and sprinted
well ahead of the shoal
down to his racing sloop,
faster salvage vessel
than that of any other
curly whiskered city elder;
and, for preaching by example,
a very hard thing as you know,
I hear received his prize.

At the end of our lives

at the end of the desert
you in a battered stetson
        a seedy tuxedo
me in a long torn black wrap
once my proud heart's black
                transparent negligee . . .

under my ex negligee my frame'll
          skitter on
under your singed bullet holes you'll stomp on
mouth to bourbon, swig passed back
        over your collapsed shoulder

I'll be screeching old Ophelia songs
             and Greensleeves
you'll be snoring the blues
      and iconoclastic notes of Bird and Monk
tapping your scraggy heels on the
                resonant pumice
sporting your old Clint and Lee
        silvered and fruity
            90 years twoday beard

while I on Marlene and Ginger ex legs
quaver my bird-light see-through hips
clear down the cactus path
        to New Mexico, New Mexico.
   Olé.

★

And there with uncontrollable hips and hands
we'll rant my boy before the great
                    bone
                              tombstone
At Albuquerque, in the desert yard
                    of that saint in earth
                    the grave gorgeous Georgia.

We will hang up our bones
for the gazing delectation and the banqueting
                    of the lovers
                              the
              circling   life
                critics   still
                    of the

And back again

Hi Miranda. Hi Arthur. I'm back.
They don't look.
Scuffling the moonlit gravel.
They wear picture book snow caps
red and blue with bobbles.
Studiously nattering, small as
they are.
           What do they say?
No answer. Mirror talk?

Under ice the water's not deep.
From the air if you leaned
from your toy plane, waving
you'd see a serpentine robe
sewn into ice, edged in a rabbit's
fur trim of snow. By night
the moonbeams avert to eyes,
Alsatians in the park, lions.
On air or by air I swing by:
my skin whips and cools.
By night the robe's
softened. I round each
         dark inlet.
Holm oak, beech, hollies
cluster like mildly
        talking crowds.
They converse around the swathed
limbs I'm overflying.
           Days
the glassy water lies in gaol.

I left the two children, quietly
pushing up into the air
with my feet, calf muscles
thigh muscles. Holding breath
after breath, hard bellied . . .

Once you have the knack
                        nothing to it

(or on the other hand
between one lake and the next
nothing: the skill cuts
                        of a sudden
goes missing, a whole life).

Now, from up hundreds of feet
the luminous water in gaol
becomes a rabbit doe's nest,
a loving mother's
                        languorous and
overspilling bed, surrounded
by tapestry leaves and small
lions couchant under the trees.

What are they talking about?
Their mirror chat. I let
my muscles relax like a net
so that
                        down I drop

            land
      without the least
   pricking of the gravel

            well
                  with such finesse
      how can they know what
            their mother was up to?

How long
I flew on high over

that melting bower, not
ruffling the leaves nor
disturbing the silver ruffed dogs
in their walk among
the moonbeams, their eyes.
In a sniff of the sound of
                  your mirror talk . . .
By the freeze in the
dark your coloured caps swing
tassles, your heads nod
to each other, two
children I call my children.
How soundless you are.

Memory: glass/ through which
I cannot push. The lake:
glass. I fly so high,
thankfully and coolly
I lose my mind in air.
Memory: glass/ through which
I cannot push. Memory:
the robed body of the lake,
how beautiful . . . how beautiful
in her melting bower

          I dropped down
               unnoticed
after the flight, behind children.
My children who stand prophesying
               on the gravel.

Autumn in Kensington Gardens
– for Michèle

Day after day the still glitter
drifts into a ragtag of leaves
and the blackbird's bobtail
scouts among the dry heaps.

We talked, intensively
comparing, of the pale gold
of the round polled trees
all up along the Broadwalk.

What kind of yellow would
you say they bore? I have
a mist memory of the ovals,
a Kate Greenaway verse book

of cutout leaves, each poised
for child's colouring, on its own
like prizes on the tree
in the middle of the winter dance.

Each one a glass lemon,
its yellow below its bumpy
glassy rind a tantalus
under my finger sliding by.

The hard lemon rolled
in my palm. I composed a
tree of fruit, a luscious golden
pear and a silver nutmeg.

And as for me I was
daughter to the Queen of Spain
and the curls on the head
of the gardener's girl

were as simple and red
as the herrings that grow in
the wood and as fat
round my right thumb

as the strawberries that swim
in shoals in the duck-
green Serpentine, at night,
when the gates are closed.

Love of babies and children

I slough each child off
every year or a couple.

1

Babies
their toes and fingers, of course perfect,
restless
helpless, but the tensile
strength coming –
The mouth
a spider movement against
my breast which is huge

We bathe in milk . . . it's the
element we share, the two of us
Her rapt bird's skull, the
skin sleek first thin plumage
My baby's whole body
held close, breathes to me
her dear perfume

And so I must too; milk
cow   But to the infant
who hasn't met
that downgraded creature
to my baby's mouth
a bird's pout

I'm wholly
the worth of warmth, of mass . . .
Rivulets, riverbrown nipples, wide yet
spraying white skeins
such as waterfalls spread out
over rocks and moss

My arms bastions to uphold

the drinker, the bird with intent eyes
sucking at each fountainhead

My shoulder a tower
to her surrender

And lastly a sound in
the beginning of darkness and sleep,
a contralto of milk   to lull

the drunken bird, a lush at her age
rose skin
                the blown skin
of, who cares?   I guard that

2

That child grows older (the
new baby comes). Our old
element stretches
between us
thinner, not without
its moments, but thinner —
                    adulterated.

The milky smell leaves
their hair slowly, then almost
from one day to the next
it's gone. You are combing
a girl or boy's hair, thick.
They pull from the comb,
complaining it's hurting
their skin.

You suppose
they get a kind of revenge,
their own back for
an absence.

Until it fades away,
with all that complaining.
You pull them towards you.
How they wriggle away
               like snakes.

Last night taking me
by my arse widened by
his fingers, he threw
himself into me and left
his head of knowledge
his perishable spirit
which I swallowed and
I think he died.
I was lucky and brave.
Then as I slept
she rose again in her
red negligee, a tank
of soldiers, a rose
a spread millefeuille bosom
a head of Pharoic wisdom
and she wanted not only
hers, but my (blue) negligee,
which I screamed at
since she had the wisdom
and my mother's rose.

'Will you spend today with her?'
She smiled with indifferent
certainty.
I wept, and behind her
a thin wand, a
beggar of two willow eyes
rose up aimlessly far off
from me. Rootlike
he moves to sneak back
inside. Why? What for?
He pleads with the pool to
root back his blue
ankle bones: 'you
cut me down.'
I don't want him.
Tears, they

moisten the ground.
Tears like this secrete him,
refresh his terrain.
Tears, they
moisten his ground.

Who will gun down
the weeping willow man,
you who are dead inside?

*Who will save me
from the willow man, the willow man?
Who will kill the willow man,
spirit inside?*

*I'll save you from
the willow man, the willow man
I'll kill the wicked willow man
but let me come outside.*

*I'll give you blood, I'll give you
back both flesh and bone
Now save me for he walks my way
the weeping willow man*

And in the morning
the intruder wanders over to me,
I lay my head on him.
Before the sun and the clock
strike, the intruder
wanders over to him, she
in sleepy warmth
lays her head on him,
she basks
on his mouth of roses.

I was in a room, in a chair.
I leant forward to see the garden.
Miranda my daughter and Alec and
then Irving moved away, talking.

Some gesticulating, a conversation
rounded and cheery. I called out
things that were sociable and pleasing
from the other side of wavering walls.

Deeper inside the house I was in such
gauzed pain I had to exist
in two rooms at once. The first,
the one I leaned from, had a wall

or no wall, a window or no
window. The other I knew of
but that room was shunned, half
dark, in further, a sawn glimpse

feinting in to mazes thought
existent in the house; mere
scratches, discolorations, markings
guessed off corners polished like

tusks, but out of focus at once.
I cast my eyes back right away.
I called to the three who were
sauntering off; my remarks brilliant.

Living in this room
of the green back garden
and the gallant canary
I take minicabs to Hampstead Heath
              and Richmond Park,
I am shored up with flowered cushions.
Sometimes I lie in the heady
coppery stems of July, uncut
          by Hampstead or Richmond.
                              Squirrels
run up the sapling trees
          of Holland Park.

I get used to
from my web, even enjoy the cans,
the sweet papers. As for
this enormous population, who
cool down on pepsis and lagers, whose
pretty children
scream outside the wall
in the day nursery, all day,
I nearly crave that frenzy.

Now   here
in the cool bottom, the moon's
          bare golden cavities
                              hide
First World hardware; and
my mother says wistfully, she
can't take pleasure in the July country
moon, a vast hunk beyond the pine trees,
any more – but only her unclipped golden yew-tree
                    on the lawn
facing out west, like a ship's maiden –

How graceful is the golden yew-tree,
seedling of my grandmother,
facing out west. How hard and golden
is the July country moon, crowded
with pickaxes, a used
vehicle lot. I said: I forget. That
doesn't worry me.

Through the dew
of her flowers, of tiger-lilies
forking through rapiers of leaves,
                    of syringas, of known
unseen petals
   we walked back
                    soft footed
each to her own considerations.

The legend of the handless queen

She has eyes like
    harebells, blue, they stare
  and mean indefinite
ecstasies. Folk say she was
   always like that, touched.
The king's son listens to
    her dumb counsel, he
  clutches her arms,
        the no handed bride,
brass coloured as ripening rye
and with gratitude for
       her clear purity, her sworn
     harebell stare, he beds
the handless queen of the rye.

Lost in a dark wood and
    searching for two children
     her babes, who float
  to the bottom of the pond
before she can cry 'no, wait!'
her stumps, groping frenziedly
    dipped in mud, grow
      slowly, muscle round bone
nerve, capillaries, skin: the ten fingers
swim like transparent roach. They
  touch her children, twine on
     their round white skulls
like weed, but to lift them.
    They gasp in her arms,
     they sick up the pond.
Her risen fingers clean their mouths and
   plant them to her.

His own hands are longstanding,
    brown, each finger
        flexible and squared
thumb pads well developed.
He has made with intricate
    sorrowing art, silver hands
        for his clear pure, sworn
bride. When she returns from
    the forest, wet and pondweed twined
        like a dead corpse
he at least can comfort her
    'your silver hands are done
        my clear bride, my one'.
She has two children clamped
    to her stumpy teats
and with her deft free hand
    throws the silver pair
        onto the roaring fire.

My middle-aged simpering and the Mystery of Mr Duncan's Maiden*

Giggling, simpering, ugh . . . I didn't however
see I was counterfeiting 'such Puberty'
such Mystery, the Maiden, 'the crystal clear brook'
that 'well of water we return to' . . . And I
the contaminator . . . In which for her father's loss
Ophelia '"the little Fertility ghost"' drowns herself;
and likewise silvery Lizzie '"drowning for an hour
or so" posed for Millais to capture a
wild chastity' . . . Wild . . . She did drown, of TB.
Water to water . . . Meanwhile, unlike Marianne
  Moore,
me again giggling and desecrator of that
inviolate field. And I thought men.

I do forget romantic men have cherished highs
about young girls who they fear to love.
'"I live in fear"' (Lawrence). O law-flame.
You and I, old Beatrice, in our bikinis, our
parti-coloured flab, should wear grave shades
and prop by the breakwater shadow
and keep our ghettoblasters low,
our horse teeth within our lips,
no 'coy glances . . . girlish attitudes'
you, bony legs up giggling, 'loathsome'.

Reminding me all of it of abysmal
uncertainty, once

    Trying To Be THE MAIDEN

                      See how
'*lovely to look at*   Modesty
imparts to her nakedness a willowy

grace . . . Bright with spring . . .
Thus Rachel' at nine years old
'a girl, lifted to Jacob's dry mouth
her cup that fed his manhood's thirst.'
No one in my teenagerhood told me
to feed Jacob's dry thirst . . . How
did I know it was the favourite
thirst and first to feed, my own a long second?
See now, it was you . . . musing along
all the time musing along
to plague me in my fat and trenchant aim,
nervy, rapid to back down.

So that I writhed   looked aside
my neck both   Swan and Leda   *chubby*
jawline imitative best as it could duck.
And skinned myself in your eye's quest
for the willowy wild grail
within my huge girlish attitude.

Water to water, cellulose to thin air
to anorexia's grace, bulimia's modesty
'Persephone showed brightness of death
her face, spring slumbering'

Later I knew it again. That 'a wife
may be maiden to the eye', by grace
of the 'watery blues and greens' of Bonnard's
bathrooms — designer Mystery of maidens!

This shrinking inviolate
you bear such love of, I went and simpered
and spoiled it or her. And let you down.
As you and yours have done to me
and mine century by century.
Our heads forced down into a bath,

a brook, some puddle.
Muddied you say by our own wallowing.
We should lie outstretched, as
'jewels innocent show in lovely depths . . .
Because it is mystery, such Puberty
counterfeited in simpering coy glances, piety
                giggles, girlish attitudes
is loathsome, contaminated water, field
    desecrated by picnickers'

Mud in your eye, Robert Duncan.

* *The poem 'The Maiden' is in Robert Duncan's first major collection,* The Opening of the Field, *1960.*

Below Lierna

'The little streams that ripple from the hills
of the green Casentin . . .'
Inferno, Canto 30

After supper we came back by the ravine.
We stopped the car in a pouch of the valley,
I being the guide – Listen –
The engine off, a white four-storeyed mill
shuttered up among the frugal acacias
a dwindled river under a stone arch
and not a growl of a dog, an owl or a wren stirring.

And not a stumbling sinner in the cleft
gnashing and splashing and grouching
'You can't just stop on the bank like that
with no lights. *Avanti*. No
I have absolutely nothing to say.
Stars through trees and a damp stream
are pretty after chianti but boring as hell
for eternity, and I come from Florence
anyway.' We drove off peacefully.

1

The scorpions come in by twos
as if to an ark, as if twining tails,
as if in the cold twilight, the end of summer
they are bored of stone, of growing colder
now in corners, and have cast
themselves as ordinary beasts
at one with the same creation
as us: unconscious they are black sores
splayed in the growing evening
on the door jamb, upside down on
the wood lintel above our entering heads.

Welcome, say the mute skull and crossbones
the dulled escutcheons
— And the *casa* teems, in its roof,
in its floor, in its woodstore downstairs
with nurseries, natural
and small as birthmarks. It takes me
all night and nightmares to rearrange
my ark and most gingerly to allow
these two only their due berth.

2

To help me you say
these two scorpions lost their way.
We go into a routine about lonely Lucifers
tied to their own tails like cans to dogs
or the other way round. There are
too many fretted ceilings to study.
Galileo would give up.

Today we are going to Camaldoli
and to see San somebody's cave, high
high before the lands slope to the Adriatic
and over the sea to Greece. I want
to get up and no further, stick
among the glowing Etruscan pines
which look soft however they scratch
squirrels. Everything is going wrong
but I rely on one thing: what I learnt
in long garish or dingy nights.
I even remember – and I want
not to do that again, but to laugh,
just as you find me (Look, behind you, a
great brown lizard, on that wall, there)
– myself literally crawling along the
corded yellow carpet screaming and moaning.

Has that to be part of my strange creation?

Has it a part? After all?
(Hiding and then advancing out like a twirler,
smiling and strychnine-happy, but damping that
down, being my happy self, *darling*?)

3

Feeble rococo! Merely I offer this:
we are both of us devil, both sunk, both have lost,
we search intensely; neither can
bear to be cause; rid it,
spray it out of our tails backward
over our shoulders. We should give each other,
shouldn't we, something more like
honey, a melting crust . . .
whatever it is the natural blessed

endow, smear yellow sweet in cruets and
make flourish in the hive . . . Our talk
is our laborious crust of honeycomb.
We hustle for simple treats and at what hour
to retract the prod . . . Can something
be made, real, that is so often,
broken, almost I'd say vigorously
and the making half spontaneous and then interrupted?

Still, you beam, the sky beams
on the house, the lizard scuds up the wall
behind a white drainpipe,
for a moment there are no shields raised,
no childhoods.
The autumn wind is softly teazing
small trees, as if we were in a fresco
grave and generous, by della Francesca.

Drinking at Ye Olde Cracke, Liverpool*

Mentally renaming it Ye Olde Pricke
of which there were some around and plenty
of young, propping up the bars or lank
outside, I took my brandy to the courtyard.

We found room by the Gents, and beyond the door,
from which light fell on damp mossed stones,
the misted moon reigned between two
squared off derelict gables, exactly between.

And to the right side of the lady our moon
way above where she rolled as round
as a golden glacé plum in a dark box
between the Vs; and higher still by ten roods

over the lighted Gentlemen, the Protestant
Cathedral pulled upright like a bear
that does not dance but hugs the city
with a blockish bulk. Slowly I nipped

your brandy, eyeing the ascending stability:
dampish, brilliant, mighty; and you went in
for more and weren't back out for decades
of din, and I warmed up to Liverpool.

* *The Beatles' pub, where John Lennon used to meet Adrian Henri;
who inspired us to visit.*

The room is Eleanor Butler

Show them to Eleanor Butler, No. 6.
And No. 7 is Sarah Ponsonby.
You show no interest, refusing me
George Borrow, who walks Wild Wales deep
in your suitcase ravine. I say
we might never be here again, in No. 6
watching a brown mallard floating
in the big Dee of many pools
and corridors and willows midstream.
Is the duck sitting comfortably? Is she in No. 6?
Eleanor Butler, for whose sake I think
I am put up here, has three graveyards
to lie in with her Beloved,
her heart's love all their lives.
Despite what people say, they weren't mice
nor poor witch women in scuttle hats.

They adored the Gothic and twice
Wellington came to visit. They tackled
the slums, twitched away at preferments,
X for chaplain, She would prefer Y
for headmaster. They sat up in the second
ceremonial barge that glided overhead the Vale
when Telford opened his Viaduct: the
short benefactresses looking down.
Into dewy mornings they gambled. Learned
as magpies they wrote their Daybooks.
The world and the Duke came riding by.

Not for his highnosed teatime grunts
nor for the kicked-back quips they laughed at
over the fat lustre pot; nor for
that cabinet of Tighes and Piozzis;
nor for the lissom improved cottage,
their vantage from which to improve the classes.
– But for their insistence, their younger

profound insistence that flowed wide
as Wordsworth might and probably said
– that flowed wide and spread outward
like the Dee over milder ground
after its fight through hard passes –
fight to have no more and no less
that this ground: E B & S P.
– For their love I do envy them.

Over the mantel to honour the Duke's
visit; it lasts and lasts; their
modest insistence. O uneasy sleeping friend,
here's love at sixes and sevens,
love as two adjoining hotel bedrooms.
How they would have chortled
and pushed off in their barge overhead.

*E B & S P: Eleanor Butler and Sarah Ponsonby inscribed their initials
over the big mantel in honour of his last visit: to their Gothic
Regency cottage, 'Plas Newydd' in Llangollen . . . as many visitors
later, including us.*

Harebell and priedieu moss by the fall.
Deeps of fir, and reed and turf green
on the high slopes, then scree and nothing
but rained out mug shots of another climb
of another hill with another, there's no sign
they're true. Anyway, bracken green
changing to bronze in the flare light,
sun after three days of rain. 'I could live here
forever,' as the grass is green by the river
and the sky is blue where I never went up
and the blackbird sings a little in the ash.

'And not a moment more' as the rain
minute by minute fills the valley
and ash, myrtle, aspen, willow,
like magpies return to black and silver,
and even the sheep – Flock by flock
they've had the use of copper mine
or slate working; the roofless cottage,
the white chimney pot on the stack on the near gable
– I find sheep in these pathetic folds, long heads
turned from the pouring fount of the south-westerlies.

           I remember
you   you fucker   and the white
sea at Cuckmere Haven.

The male attendant
holds out a robe.
He gives a V sign
as the Queen of Sheba
trembly and spangly
steps from the milk of the Channel.
A two sailed ship passes.
Into a broad slipway that expands
between the crescents of the water
and the clarity of sky (*that's*
the sky) . . . a light
in which horizons drift loose,
where dimensions unfasten,
a whiteness that Sheba's eye
hits with wonder, returns to
with exasperated wonder . . .
Within the collar of silver
neither sea nor sky are harnessed really at all.

Yet it broadens, broadens,
it snags in crabs, cormorants,
a ghost ship, a spirit
splashing by the water's edge.
Until the sun goes down
and she goes with him
back, trudging
over the piled shingle breakwater.

                                        ★

Lady and playboy
they tuck into their barouche
of flowing silver, inside which
they instantly dispute and disagree
over anything and everything as
they skitter and rumble homeward;
once, in their heat, tipping out into
the cowfield, what with his tickling
and her poopoohing . . .
no one could claim much for this pair.

       ★

Into the broad slipway
    the boat sails

A spit of rock as the tide sinks
    down   uncurls from
        the chalk cliff   like

a dark bar of cloud
    Above   below, the slipway
a curved dazzle   loosened   far

    floating   the mast
      peters around the rock as if
      floating